Oxford Reading Tree

Floppy's Phonics

Level 5

Activity Book 5

Debbie Hepplewhite

OXFORD

Practise the sound

/ai/

ai
wait
plain
main
afraid
rained
complaint

-ay
away
play
tray
player
layers
dismayed

eigh
weigh
eight
neigh
sleigh
weight
eighteen

-ey
they
grey
osprey
prey
survey
convey

Read the words in each spelling word bank. Underline all the different spellings for the /ai/ sound. Can you think of more words for each word bank?

Now that I'm eight, I can go on my sister May's sleigh. It is pulled by her sweet horse, Grey. Look at his plain brown coat and hear his neigh. I can play with Grey in the sun and rain.

Read the text. Underline all the different spellings for the /ai/ sound.

Write a short sentence and draw a picture to illustrate it.

Practise the sound

/ai/

a-e
made
game
take
grapes
scrape
escape

a
apron
baby
lady
acorn
table
April

-ae
sundae
reggae
Gaelic
Mae
Rae

-ea
break
great
steak
windbreaker
greatest

Read the words in each spelling word bank. Underline all the different spellings for the /ai/ sound. Can you think of more words for each word bank?

The lady had her baby late in April. The baby was given the name Jade Mae. It was the same name as her amazing great-grandmother!

Read the text. Underline all the different spellings for the /ai/ sound.

Write a short sentence and draw a picture to illustrate it.

Practise the sound

/ee/

ee
deep
steep
creep
street
weekend
free

-y
funny
rainy
windy
stormy
lucky
luckily

e
me
she
emu
equals
behave
sequins

-ey
key
donkey
turkey
valley
parsley
trolley

Read the words in each spelling word bank. Underline all the different spellings for the /ee/ sound. Can you think of more words for each word bank?

Last weekend was rainy, with frequent stormy showers. It was too windy to go out. Luckily, we could stay in and play with Grandad. He made us yummy turkey bake with leeks for dinner.

Read the text. Underline all the different spellings for the /ee/ sound.

Write a short sentence and draw a picture to illustrate it.

Practise the sound

-ie
field
brief
thief
chief
shield
fiend

ea
teach
leaf
leaves
leave
reach
stream

e-e
eve
swede
compete
complete
extremely
stampede

Read the words in each spelling word bank. Underline all the different spellings for the /ee/ sound. Can you think of more words for each word bank?

The teacher was eating a piece of peach when a thief ran off with his briefcase. The thief ran away extremely quickly across the field and fell in a stream. He shrieked!

Read the text. Underline all the different spellings for the /ee/ sound.

Write a short sentence and draw a picture to illustrate it.

Practise the sound

/igh/

-igh
sigh
flight
bright
lightning
brighten
slightly

-y
why
cry
shy
flying
magnify
reply

i
find
kind
minus
behind
child
remind

Read the words in each spelling word bank. Underline all the different spellings for the /igh/ sound. Can you think of more words for each word bank?

The mighty king had a fight with a wild flying dragon. Suddenly, the dragon was blinded by a flash of lightning. The kind king ran behind the dragon to rescue his shy child.

Read the text. Underline all the different spellings for the /igh/ sound.

Write a short sentence and draw a picture to illustrate it.

Practise the sound

/igh/

-ie

tied
cries
dries
flies
replied
identified

i-e

line
wipe
like
stripes
strides
inside

Read the words in each spelling word bank. Underline all the different spellings for the /igh/ sound. Can you think of more words for each word bank?

Lyla gave a smile as she tried to find the needle to finish the stripes on the quilt. Her mother began it which is why Lyla prized it.

Read the text. Underline all the different spellings for the /igh/ sound.

Write a short sentence and draw a picture to illustrate it.

Practise the sound

oa

soap
loaf
toasted
poached
groan
foaming

ow

grown
flow
throw
blowing
window
fellow

o

oval
hello
most
older
both
mango

Read the words in each spelling word bank. Underline all the different spellings for the /oa/ sound. Can you think of more words for each word bank?

A shoal of bold fish darted near the old rowing boat as it floated slowly along the coastline towing a net. The low setting sun made a golden glow over the sea.

Read the text. Underline all the different spellings for the /oa/ sound.

Write a short sentence and draw a picture to illustrate it.

Practise the sound

/oa/

oe

toe
doe
foes
oboe
hoe
goes

o-e

code
home alone
ear lobe
awoke
globe
throne

-ough

dough
though
although

-eau

plateau
gateau
chateau
bureau

Read the words in each spelling word bank. Underline all the different spellings for the /oa/ sound. Can you think of more words for each word bank?

The doe trotted across the plateau close to my home. As the sun rose, I awoke. I took a doughnut and a gateau, and crept up to the doe on tiptoe.

Read the text. Underline all the different spellings for the /oa/ sound.

Write a short sentence and draw a picture to illustrate it.

8

Practise the sound

-se
purse
horse
sense
nurse
grease
loose

-ce
voice
fleece
mice
pounce
peaceful
force

s
sunset
sunshine
slipper
silly
silver
post

-ss
kiss
cross
press
lessons
missing
dressing gown

Read the words in each spelling word bank. Underline all the different spellings for the /s/ sound. Can you think of more words for each word bank?

Write a short sentence and draw a picture to illustrate it.

One of the ugly sisters ran away from the prince's footman. She had tried to force the tiny slipper on to her big foot – but it didn't fit! She was cross. She ran across the yard to find her horse.

Read the text. Underline all the different spellings for the /s/ sound.

Practise the sound

ce
cellar
cent
December
celebrate
centipede

ci
city
circus
cinema
exercise
decide

cy
icy
bicycle
life cycle
fancy
policy

Read the words in each spelling word bank. Underline all the different spellings for the /s/ sound. Can you think of more words for each word bank?

Write a short sentence and draw a picture to illustrate it.

Cinderella felt that her hopes and dreams were fanciful. At the same time, the footman raced across the city to celebrate the exciting happenings with the prince.

Read the text. Underline all the different spellings for the /s/ sound.

Practise the sound

/s/

sc

scent

scene

scenic

scientist

scenery

discern

-st-

thistle

castle

whistle

listen

f<u>a</u>sten

hasten

Read the words in each spelling word bank. Underline all the different spellings for the /s/ sound. Can you think of more words for each word bank?

Write a short sentence and draw a picture to illustrate it.

The crown rested amongst the spiky thistles in the field. The princess spied something glistening in the sunlight. She decided to hasten down the castle steps to the scene below.

Read the text. Underline all the different spellings for the /s/ sound.

Practise the sound

/e/

e

enter

exit

exist

spend

shelter

excellent

-ea

bread

steady

ready

weather

spread

feathers

Read the words in each spelling word bank. Underline all the different spellings for the /e/ sound. Can you think of more words for each word bank?

The weather turned wet and wild. The angry wind and clouds spread east. The rain fell heavily on the window panes. Inside, we sheltered next to the fire and spread jam on our bread. We rested our heads on feather pillows.

Read the text. Underline all the different spellings for the /e/ sound.

Write a short sentence and draw a picture to illustrate it.

Practise the sound

/j/

j
jam jar
ajar
juggle
jester
jagged
jutting out

ge
gem
germs
gentle
gemstone
emergency
gentleman

gi
giant
origin
digits
fragile
ginger
gigantic

gy
stingy
energy
spongy
dingy
allergy
apology

Read the words in each spelling word bank. Underline all the different spellings for the /j/ sound. Can you think of more words for each word bank?

Write a short sentence and draw a picture to illustrate it.

That little ginger kitten, Jet, has so much energy. He is not at all gentle. You had better hide away your jam jars and fragile ornaments!

Read the text. Underline all the different spellings for the /j/ sound.

Practise the sound

/j/

-dge

edge

badge

hedge

smudged

sledge

porridge

-ge

barge

large

emerge

vill<u>age</u>

sponge

arrange

Read the words in each spelling word bank. Underline all the different spellings for the /j/ sound. Can you think of more words for each word bank?

The children jumped up and emerged from the room when the bell rang. They dodged, jostled and nudged to grab the large box. It had a strange stamp on it with red ink smudged across the edge.

Read the text. Underline all the different spellings for the /j/ sound.

Write a short sentence and draw a picture to illustrate it.

Practise the sound

-le

table

single

bottle

uncle

angle

settle

Read the words in each spelling word bank. Underline all the different spellings for the /ul/ sound. Can you think of more words for each word bank?

-el

label

parcel

camel

tunnel

travel

towel

Little Tom was always willing and able to help. He did not have a single idle bone in his body. Mabel, his big sister, sent him parcels when she travelled which she labelled, 'To Tom Gable – the Greatest'.

Read the text. Underline all the different spellings for the /ul/ sound.

Write a short sentence and draw a picture to illustrate it.

© Oxford University Press © Phonics International Ltd. 2020

Practise the sound

/ul/

-al

final

equal

signal

vertical

horizontal

hospital

-il

fossil

pencil

evil

nostrils

stencil

civil

Read the words in each spelling word bank. Underline all the different spellings for the /ul/ sound. Can you think of more words for each word bank?

My dad liked looking for, and digging for, fossils. He had land-animal fossils and sea-animal fossils. He liked the horizontal and vertical patterns on them.

Read the text. Underline all the different spellings for the /ul/ sound.

Write a short sentence and draw a picture to illustrate it.

Practise the sound

/yoo/

u

tens and units

uniform

united

computer

human

ambulance

Read the words in each spelling word bank. Underline all the different spellings for the /yoo/ sound. Can you think of more words for each word bank?

-ue

due

value

venue

Tuesday

argue

rescue

The venue for the barbecue is the park. It is next Tuesday. This is long overdue and will be a great way to unite the town. The tickets are good value and it will be lots of fun!

Read the text. Underline all the different spellings for the /yoo/ sound.

Write a short sentence and draw a picture to illustrate it.

Practise the sound

/yoo/

ew

new

few

news

dew

mildew

newborn

u-e

cube

tubes

cute

sand dunes

amused

attitude

eu

feud

Europe

eucalyptus

neutral

Read the words in each spelling word bank. Underline all the different spellings for the /yoo/ sound. Can you think of more words for each word bank?

Stew and Matthew had an argument over using the computer. Matthew was not amused! Stew, however, had a kind attitude. He let Matthew finish his unit on 'Feudal England' and went to read the newspaper!

Read the text. Underline all the different spellings for the /yoo/ sound.

Write a short sentence and draw a picture to illustrate it.

Practise the sound

oo

loom

boots

marooned

cocoon

cockatoo

stoops

u-e

rules

flute

plume

prunes

pollute

para<u>chu</u>te

-o

move

improve

movie

prove

to do

<u>who</u>

-ou-

you

soup

group

wound

ro<u>u</u>te

coupon

Read the words in each spelling word bank. Underline all the different spellings for the long /oo/ sound. Can you think of more words for each word bank?

Oona's mum was very astute. "Oona," she said. "I think that you need a break. Take these coupons and a group of pals, and go to see a movie."

Read the text. Underline all the different spellings for the long /oo/ sound.

Write a short sentence and draw a picture to illustrate it.

© Oxford University Press © Phonics International Ltd. 2020

Practise the sound

long /oo/

-ue
blue
clue
true
glue
rue
gluestick

-ew
brew
strewn
shrew
shrewd
flew
threw

-ui
suit
fruit
suitcase
juice
juicy
grapefruit

-u
super
truly
unruly
fluid
flu
ruling

Read the words in each spelling word bank. Underline all the different spellings for the long /oo/ sound. Can you think of more words for each word bank?

Write a short sentence and draw a picture to illustrate it.

The new recruit has proved to be suitable. The last recruit was clueless about safety rules. He threw his rubbish on the table and we had plumes of smoke polluting the room when he used the fruit juicer!

Read the text. Underline all the different spellings for the long /oo/ sound.

Practise the sound

/oi/

oi

soil

coin

toiled

joins

ointment

appointment

oy

joyful

enjoyment

convoy

employer

employee

destroyed

Read the words in each spelling word bank. Underline all the different spellings for the /oi/ sound. Can you think of more words for each word bank?

The heavy rain nearly spoilt the children's party, but they moved the toys inside. They had music and games and a huge toy box! The children enjoyed the party.

Read the text. Underline all the different spellings for the /oi/ sound.

Write a short sentence and draw a picture to illustrate it.

Practise the sound

/ou/

ow

bow
frown
clown
power
shower
crowd

ou

spout
proud
clouds
bountiful
spouse
round

-ough

plough
bough
drought

Read the words in each spelling word bank. Underline all the different spellings for the /ou/ sound. Can you think of more words for each word bank?

North, east, south and west, we have a bountiful land. We plough the fields, plant the forests, trek up the hills and sail the seas. Thanks to plenty of sunshine and showers of rain, we can also be proud of our rich farmland.

Read the text. Underline all the different spellings for the /ou/ sound.

Write a short sentence and draw a picture to illustrate it.

Practise the sound

or

worn

torn

sporty

cornet

forty

shortened

-our

your

four

pour

of course

downpour

resources

Read the words in each spelling word bank. Underline all the different spellings for the /or/ sound. Can you think of more words for each word bank?

The source of the problem was the stormy weather. Of course April showers were normal and to be expected. This year, however, the downpour went on for forty days in a row! All sport had to be cancelled.

Read the text. Underline all the different spellings for the /or/ sound.

Write a short sentence and draw a picture to illustrate it.

Practise the sound

aw
draw

prawns

straws

law courts

coleslaw

tawny owl

au
haul

sauce

saucer

pause

haunt

August

-al
all

hall

walk tall

stalk

chalks

called

war
war

wart

warm

warning

wardrobe

towards

Read the words in each spelling word bank. Underline all the different spellings for the /or/ sound. Can you think of more words for each word bank?

We had fun in the warm sunshine, drawing on the pavement with chalk. Then there was a rain storm, so we had to pause. Mum called us in and poured us a warming drink.

Read the text. Underline all the different spellings for the /or/ sound.

Write a short sentence and draw a picture to illustrate it.

24

Practise the sound

ur

surf
slurp
sturdy
burst
turnip
burgers

ir

dirty
squirm
birthday
confirm
swirling
thirsty

er

germ
verbs
herbal tea
germinate
permanent
thermometer

Read the words in each spelling word bank. Underline all the different spellings for the /ur/ sound. Can you think of more words for each word bank?

Write a short sentence and draw a picture to illustrate it.

Bert likes to surf. He went surfing on his birthday in the swirling waves. He squirmed when he found out that I put herbal tea in his bottle for him to slurp when he gets thirsty!

Read the text. Underline all the different spellings for the /ur/ sound.

Practise the sounds

ear	wor	-re	-our
early	work	centre	colour
learn	words	litre	rumour
search	world	metre	humour
pearls	worst	fibres	favour
heard	worth	acre	savour
rehearse	earthworm	ogre	flavour

Read the words in each spelling word bank. Underline all the different spellings for the /ur/ sound (**ear** and **or**) and schwa /u/ sound (**re** and **our**). Can you think of more words for each word bank?

Write a short sentence and draw a picture to illustrate it.

Early one morning the giant ogre awoke to search for earthworms. He heard a rumour that the worms which were pink in colour were the worst in the world, so he set to work looking for brown ones. Soon he had a five litre bucket of worms to savour. It was worth it!

Read the text. Underline all the different spellings for the /ur/ sound (**ear** and **or**) and schwa /u/ sound (**re** and **our**).

26

Practise the sound

/u/

u
ugly
jungle
jumper
thunder
understand
unbelievable

o
money
other
brother
sponge
London
wonderful

-ou
touch
couple
flourish
double
trouble
touching

-ough
borough
thorough
thoroughly
thoroughfare

Read the words in each spelling word bank. Underline all the different spellings for the /u/ sound. Can you think of more words for each word bank?

We jumped on the train to London. We walked down a thoroughfare, and I saw a huge tower block that must have cost a lot of money. We went home thinking the city was an ugly concrete jungle.

Read the text. Underline all the different spellings for the /u/ sound.

Write a short sentence and draw a picture to illustrate it.

Practise the sound

/ar/

ar

smart

artist

farmer

market

partridge

depart

al

half, halves

calf, calves

palm

calmly

balmy

palm tree

a

father

rather

lather

banana

drama

llama

Read the words in each spelling word bank. Underline all the different spellings for the /ar/ sound. Can you think of more words for each word bank?

My father would rather buy a partridge from the farmer at the market than go to the smart supermarket. My mother and younger brother prefer the calm supermarket to the drama and buzz of the market stall.

Read the text. Underline all the different spellings for the /ar/ sound.

Write a short sentence and draw a picture to illustrate it.

28

Practise the sound

-s

measure

pleasure

treasure

leisure

casualty

unusual

-si

vision

television

division

invasion

confusion

illusion

-ge

collage

montage

deluge

barrage

Read the words in each spelling word bank. Underline all the different spellings for the /zh/ sound. Can you think of more words for each word bank?

Write a short sentence and draw a picture to illustrate it.

On the television, they reported that treasure had been found in a car park! There was confusion at first about who had found it. The expert they talked to said, "It fills me with pleasure to see this treasure". I made a collage to record the unusual events.

Read the text. Underline all the different spellings for the /zh/ sound.

Practise the sound

/w/

w

cobweb
wicked
wellies
westerly
earwig
wobbly

wh

which <u>one</u>
wheel
whelk
whisper
whistle

-u

penguin
suite
persuade
persuasion

Read the words in each spelling word bank. Underline all the different spellings for the /w/ sound. Can you think of more words for each word bank?

The princess wiped the cobwebs from her wellies and set off to find the prince. He was whistling and watching an earwig crawl up a wheel. In a whisper she tried to persuade him of her plan.

Read the text. Underline all the different spellings for the /w/ sound.

Write a short sentence and draw a picture to illustrate it.

Practise the sound

/f/

f
café
trifle
fantastic
feather
floating
flamingo

Read the words in each spelling word bank. Underline all the different spellings for the /f/ sound. Can you think of more words for each word bank?

-ff
puffin
raffle
traffic
coffee
different
difficult

I met Fiona in the café for a coffee. She was wearing a flamingo print scarf which floated around her neck. She looked fantastic. She said she won it in a raffle. All I have ever won is a trifle!

Read the text. Underline all the different spellings for the /f/ sound.

Write a short sentence and draw a picture to illustrate it.

Practise the sound

/f/

ph

telephone

paragraph

photograph

elephant

dolphin

nephew

-gh

rough

tough

enough

co<u>ugh</u>

roughly

la<u>ugh</u>ter

Read the words in each spelling word bank. Underline all the different spellings for the /f/ sound. Can you think of more words for each word bank?

Bob the elephant had a phone call from his rough, tough nephew, Phil. Phil was a photographer. He offered to take a photograph of Bob and his pal Steph, a dolphin.

Read the text. Underline all the different spellings for the /f/ sound.

Write a short sentence and draw a picture to illustrate it.

Practise the sounds

/ch/ **/sh/** **/k/**

ch as code for /ch/

child

children

charity

cherish

branches

choose

ch as code for /sh/

machine

chute

parachute

chiffon

chef

ch as code for /k/

school

character

chemist

chameleon

stomach

Read the words in each spelling word bank. Underline all the different pronunciations for the grapheme **ch**. Can you think of more words for each word bank?

At school, the children were raising money for charity. They did a play about chameleons parachuting from the jungle branches. Each child was a different character in the play, but they all wore chiffon outfits.

Read the text. Underline all the different pronunciations for the grapheme **ch**.

Write a short sentence and draw a picture to illustrate it.

Practise the sounds

/igh/ /ee/

ie as code for /igh/

replies
pies
magnified
identified
shied away
horrified

ie as code for /ee/

niece
windshield
showpiece
hygienic
make-believe
relief

ie as code for /ee/
(at the end of some words)

pixie
movie
cookie
rookie
freebie

Read the words in each spelling word bank. Underline all the different pronunciations for the grapheme **ie**. Can you think of more words for each word bank?

My niece took me to the cinema. The movie was make-believe with an evil fairy and a horrified pixie. It is the sort of film I have shied away from in the past but it was a freebie so I went along. It was a huge relief when it ended.

Read the text. Underline all the different pronunciations for the grapheme **ie**.

Write a short sentence and draw a picture to illustrate it.

Practise the sounds

/ou/

/oa/

ow as code for /ou/

flowers

crown

powder

howls

growled

down town

Read the words in each spelling word bank. Underline all the different pronunciations for each word bank?

ow as code for /oa/

owner

below

bellow

sorrow

slowly

tomorrow

The powder puff made the children howl with laughter. I gave my niece a crown of flowers but then the shop owner growled so I put it back. We will go down town again tomorrow.

Read the text. Underline all the different pronunciations for the grapheme **ow**.

Write a short sentence and draw a picture to illustrate it.

© Oxford University Press © Phonics International Ltd. 2020

Practise the sounds

/a/   /o/   /ai/

a as code for /a/

adder
acrobat
rabbit
animal
paddle
actually

wa as code for /o/

was
wash
what
swallow
wander
swan

a as code for /ai/

tasty
wasteful
danger
bathe
gravy
lady, ladies

Read the words in each spelling word bank. Underline all the different pronunciations for the grapheme **a**. Can you think of more words for each word bank?

Write a short sentence and draw a picture to illustrate it.

It was sunny on Saturday, so the ladies went to the farm. They wandered around and saw baby rabbits washing themselves and lambs hopping happily.

Read the text. Underline all the different pronunciations for the grapheme **a**.

Practise the sounds

/ch/	
/chu/	

ch

bench

parchment

chick

drenched

attached

cherish

-tch

batch

kitchen

crutches

watchtower

thatch

scratched

-ture

nature

features

adventure

departure

creatures

furniture

Read the words in each spelling word bank. Underline all the different spellings for the /ch/ sound and /chu/ sound. Can you think of more words for each word bank?

The adventure began on a park bench. I met a man with a briefcase attached to his arm. There was a piece of parchment inside the case with a map scratched on the surface. The man said the map showed where the treasure was. We must prepare for departure at once.

Read the text. Underline all the different spellings for the /ch/ sound and /chu/ sound.

Write a short sentence and draw a picture to illustrate it.

Practise the sound

/sh/

sh

shallow

shapes

shopping

wishes

shoot

shivering

Read the words in each spelling word bank. Underline all the different spellings for the /sh/ sound. Can you think of more words for each word bank?

ch

chef

chute

chaperone

chivalry

chiffon

parachute

The chef went shopping. She needed a new dishwasher, and a chute to send dirty dishes to the sink. She found them both – her wishes had come true!

Read the text. Underline all the different spellings for the /sh/ sound.

Write a short sentence and draw a picture to illustrate it.

Practise the sound

-ti

station

initials

essential

mention

position

invitation

-ci

special

delicious

ancient

artificial

social

politician

-ssi

mission

expressions

discussion

procession

compassion

permission

-sci

unconscious

conscious

conscience

Read the words in each spelling word bank. Underline all the different spellings for the /sh/ sound. Can you think of more words for each word bank?

The brothers met at the bus station. They were conscious that they had to find outfits for a special party quickly. There was much discussion on the bus, then success at the shops!

Read the text. Underline all the different spellings for the /sh/ sound.

Write a short sentence and draw a picture to illustrate it.

Practise the sound

g

gold
greenhouse
glass
gardening
group
great

gu

guess
guest
guard
guitar
guide
disguise

-gue

league
rogue
plague
catalogue
dialogue
colleague

gh

ghost
ghetto
gherkin
ghastly
ghost town
ghostwriter

Read the words in each spelling word bank. Underline all the different spellings for the /g/ sound. Can you think of more words for each word bank?

The gardening club met in the greenhouse after school. They looked in the catalogue to choose the next plants. The last lot had been destroyed by a rogue plague of aphids. The group was very keen to come top of the league and win the gold gherkin trophy.

Read the text. Underline all the different spellings for the /g/ sound.

Write a short sentence and draw a picture to illustrate it.

Practise the sound

/eer/

eer	ear	-ere	-ier
cheers	hears	here	pier
eerie	appear	yours sincerely	skier
pioneer	a clearing	hemisphere	tiers
mutineer	fear	severe	pierce
engineer	yearly	adhere	fierce
veneer	gears	persevere	cashier

Read the words in each spelling word bank. Underline all the different spellings for the /eer/ sound. Can you think of more words for each word bank?

I shook with fear. I could hear an eerie sound. Suddenly, a fierce tiger appeared in the forest clearing. Its fierce growls and piercing claws made me feel sheer terror. However, I persevered, and in the end it ran away. I cheered!

Read the text. Underline all the different spellings for the /eer/ sound.

Write a short sentence and draw a picture to illustrate it.

Practise the sound

/air/

air
flair
fairy
hairy
pair
repair
chairperson

-are
share
square
flares
scarecrow
declare
spare parts

-ear
bear
pears
swear
tearing
footwear
unbearable

-ere
there
where
nowhere
somewhere
everywhere
premiere

Read the words in each spelling word bank. Underline all the different spellings for the /air/ sound. Can you think of more words for each word bank?

Write a short sentence and draw a picture to illustrate it.

The chairperson of the premier league football team declared that the star player was a 'spare part' to the club. He said it was unbearable to watch his lack of flair on the field. The player replied that it was all down to unsuitable footwear.

Read the text. Underline all the different spellings for the /air/ sound.

Practise the sound

n	kn	-nn	gn
number	knot	funny	gnaw
nine	know	bonnet	gnome
never	knee	punnet	gnat
even	knight	stunning	gnawing
night	knitting	runner	sign
hundred	knife	spanner	design

Read the words in each spelling word bank. Underline all the different spellings for the /n/ sound. Can you think of more words for each word bank?

The stunning runner was on track to take first place until he injured his knee. He gnawed and gnashed his teeth and finally threw himself over the hundred metre line to come in at number nine. This was his best effort but he knew his best days were over.

Read the text. Underline all the different spellings for the /n/ sound.

Write a short sentence and draw a picture to illustrate it.

Practise the sound

r

register
ruler
rap music
already
right
ruby ring

wr

wrist
wren
wreck
wrap
wrong
write

Read the words in each spelling word bank. Underline all the different spellings for the /r/ sound. Can you think of more words for each word bank?

-rr

arrive
arrival
arrow
hurry
sorry
carrot

rh

rhyme
rhythm
rhubarb
rhinoceros
rhapsody

When I arrived I was in a hurry to register for the event. I wrapped a band around my right wrist and asked my friend to write my name on for me. The rap music was so loud but to me, it was a fabulous rhapsody of rhyme.

Read the text. Underline all the different spellings for the /r/ sound.

Write a short sentence and draw a picture to illustrate it.

Practise the sound

m

merit
marbles
magnificent
submerge
camera
dream

-mb

comb
lamb
plumber
limbs
climb
thumb

-mn

autumn
solemn
column
condemn
solemnly
columns

-mm

immense
hammer
immediate
summer
swimmer
shimmering

Read the words in each spelling word bank. Underline all the different spellings for the /m/ sound. Can you think of more words for each word bank?

I had a magnificent dream. It was summer and I sat by a shimmering pool to watch the long limbs of a swimmer slice the water while I ran a comb through my hair. Then an immense hammer came down and I solemnly woke up to autumn.

Read the text. Underline all the different spellings for the /m/ sound.

Write a short sentence and draw a picture to illustrate it.

Practise the sound

/k/

k	-ck	c
kangaroo	rocket	caravan
king	packing	crisps
kite	socks	cattle
skittles	duckling	cargo
keyhole	trickle	clarinet
skips	blocks	clothes

Read the words in each spelling word bank. Underline all the different spellings for the /k/ sound. Can you think of more words for each word bank?

I was playing with a pack of cards in the caravan while my sister practised her clarinet. The cattle outside seemed to be confused by the kite which was tangled in the clothes line. The cows kept mooing and my sister kept blowing. The noise was dreadful!

Read the text. Underline all the different spellings for the /k/ sound.

Write a short sentence and draw a picture to illustrate it.

Practise the sound

ch

chorus

chords

orchestra

monarch

architect

qu

mosquito

conquer

mannequin

marquee

que

antique

cheque

plaque

picturesque

grotesque

Read the words in each spelling word bank. Underline all the different spellings for the /k/ sound. Can you think of more words for each word bank?

It was a fantastic venue in a picturesque setting. As the orchestra struck the first chord, the singers raised their voices in a loud chorus. At the end they collected coins and cheques for charity.

Read the text. Underline all the different spellings for the /k/ sound.

Write a short sentence and draw a picture to illustrate it.

Practise the sound

or	-ore	-our	-oor	oar
port	pores (skin)	pour	door	soar (fly)
fort	store	fourteen	poor	roars
orbit	seashore	course	floor	board
sportswoman	explore	court	outdoors	hoarse
tornado	sore	resourceful	poorly	coarse
horse	bored	fourth	moor	overboard

Read the words in each spelling word bank. Underline all the different spellings for the /or/ sound. Can you think of more words for each word bank?

The resourceful sportswoman hit the ball into orbit. I watched it soar out of centre court! The crowds were hoarse from their roars of disbelief. Of course her opponent thought the spectators went overboard with their response.

Read the text. Underline all the different spellings for the /or/ sound.

Write a short sentence and draw a picture to illustrate it.

Practise the sound

aw
fawn
gnaw
crawl
lawn
strawberries
trawler

-al
small
walk
ball
stalls
falling
tallest

au
automatic
applause
pause
saucer
nautical
haul

Read the words in each spelling word bank. Underline all the different spellings for the /or/ sound. Can you think of more words for each word bank?

The crowd burst into automatic applause at the sight of the small fawn on the lawn. As we munched our strawberries, we felt guilty because we had startled the poor fawn.

Read the text. Underline all the different spellings for the /or/ sound.

Write a short sentence and draw a picture to illustrate it.

Practise the sound

/or/

-augh
taught
caught
daughter
haughty
naughty
granddaughter

Read the words in each spelling word bank. Underline all the different spellings for the /or/ sound. Can you think of more words for each word bank?

ough
nought
ought
bought
brought
thought
fought

I caught my naughty daughter cutting her doll's hair. My mother had brought that doll for her granddaughter and would not be pleased about the haircut. I thought it best not to mention it, so I hid the doll and bought another one.

Read the text. Underline all the different spellings for the /or/ sound.

Write a short sentence and draw a picture to illustrate it.

Oxford Reading Tree

Floppy's Phonics

Oxford Level 5

Activity Book 5

Say the sounds and practise your reading, spelling and handwriting skills.

Text © Oxford University Press
© Phonics International Ltd 2020

Illustrations by Oxford Designers and Illustrators

Cover Illustration by Alex Brychta

The characters in this work are the original creation of Roderick Hunt and Alex Brychta who retain copyright in the characters.

First published 2011
This edition published 2020

ISBN 978-1-38-200560-9

10 9 8 7
Printed in China

Paper used in the production of this book is a natural, recyclable product made from wood grown in sustainable forests. The manufacturing process conforms to the environmental regulations of the country of origin.

Oxford OWL
Helping your child's learning with free eBooks, essential tips and fun activities
www.oxfordowl.co.uk

OXFORD UNIVERSITY PRESS
₹195.₀₀

OXFORD
UNIVERSITY PRESS

How to get in touch:
web www.oxfordprimary.co.uk
email primary.enquiries@oup.com
tel. +44 (0) 1536 452610
fax +44 (0) 1865 313472

ISBN 978-1-38-200560-9

9 781382 005609